what forever feels like

fragile heart
book three

celia sinclair

e.m. handly

Two Ten Press

E.M. Handly
writing as
Celia Sinclair

Two Ten Press
twotenpress@gmail.com

eBook ISBN: 979-8-9887211-4-7
Print ISBN: 979-8-9887211-5-4

www.emhandly.com

*To my 'ride or die', it's a shame
you never loved me, for me…*

contents

You wanted to cage me, but I am untamed…

blinded

somehow you've managed
to stitch together the fragments
of my broken heart...

~ *patches*

I told you I'd follow you
anywhere

and I meant it

god I hate writing on the
left side of a journal
it's as awkward
as us

if opportunity presented itself
I would go
for you

but then comes a sign

a little bit of faith
renewed

~ don't wanna leave here

he flounders
and stutters
frustratingly silent
never knows
the perfect words to say

he's misunderstood
and hard to love
even harder to put up with
but he's loyal

he protects me
loves me
gives *all of himself*
to me

I am his
he is mine
never dream
of going astray

~ *forever*

your gaze burned a hole
in my heart

the corner of my perception
capturing — something

hiding — waiting — wanting

I could read your thoughts
feel your soul

your inner most postures
surfaced

long enough for me to know
I am right where I should be

~ hello you

I bought you one of
my favorite books
I mean, you like to read
right

you turned me onto
many classics
and I read them
all of them

conversations with god
made me think differently
spiritually
it was invigorating

you said I was a horrible
gift giver and you
would never read it

told me I obviously
don't know you or listen
'cause you don't believe in god

I tried to explain
it wasn't that kinda book

~ *didn't matter*

sometimes I think you can feel

I know this because sometimes
I feel you

I wish the passion you had for your art
would give me the same attention

then again
I take what I can get

sometimes I think your mine
and other times...
it seems you never wanted
to be committed

six years later, I still wait...

~ *why*

6:30 am
shower and put on
my happy face

drop the kids off at school
then off to my stimulating 9-5
to sit in my cubicle and stare
at the computer for the day

4:00 pm
a sigh of relief
pick up the kids, go home
sit for a moment with a cocktail
to unwind

time to start dinner
gosh is it so late already
gotta pack everyone's lunch
get my coffee ready

the dog is whining for his walk
and I wonder if it's Friday yet

~ 21st century wife

dear diary

it always feels so much better
starting off with a greeting

makes the mind believe
someone is actually listening

or should I say
eventually read this

the greatest mind trick

he hasn't spoke to me
since dinner yesterday

other than brush off
my attempted conversation with
I'm busy

I still have no idea why
he's so angry with me
par for the course

his anger and words
have always hurt
but for some reason

his silence *kills* me

I wonder if this is normal
for other couples

I wonder how many women lie awake
in their beds silently weeping
or sneak tears in the tub

will love always be
so painful

what happened to the purity
of it all — the sanity
the longevity

it is so lonely only writing to you
but there's no one left
to listen

~ *what the fuck did I do*

as you love me
with your eyes
sharing your desires
I stare out the window
at the big pine

the demons dance
inside my head
devouring anything
encouraging

stomping
laughing
twirling

having a feast
with my thoughts

~ *uninterested*

the shower cleanses my soul
of the driver with road rage
and the hillbilly neighbor
who has made a habit
of knocking on our door
for a cigarette

cotton candy suds in my hair
reminding me of everything
that is good in the world

knowing I'll soon
feel everything that is
good in the world

put on your favorite t-shirt
with the three-quarter sleeves
that shows you when I'm cold
makes you want to kiss them

braid my hair just like you like
admire myself in the mirror

walk through the house
half-naked just to tease you

patiently waiting for you
escape to our sacred place
all our own
just for us

~ saturday

It's been hard to love you.
But I know it isn't easy loving me.

At your side I am a Goddess.
We're going to conquer worlds.

I've been here
through all of it

the sadness
the pain

the conceit
only to be
humbled

the success
the epic failure

the self-inflicted
unnecessary
heartache and stress

I've been here
through it *all*
and I'm still here

then I realized
you weren't lazy
you simply
lacked gratitude

~ nothing I can do

I am not here
to be anyone's beckon call
I spread myself as wide as I can

kids — husband
extended family

but goddamn it
I am still me

I get a fucking slice
of that pie

~ too tired

to have youth
is to know everything
and yet remain
so helpless
vulnerable
naive

so willing to
love and sacrifice

you must endure the pain
of having your heart
broke a time or two
before you can truly
appreciate how wonderful
it feels to be whole

but *am* I

~ *whole*

you are frustratingly
exhausting

riding my patience
like a razor teasing the
edge of a piece of paper

ignorantly temperamental

extracting every ounce
of optimism with your
negative syphon

~ please stop

you can be cold
relentlessly closed off

yet sometimes your
vulnerability floats

like dandelion tufts
through the air

in the forced breath
of a child

~ momentarily fragile

your razor thin tongue
took another slice
of respect today

that monster you feed
is always hungry

I strategize how to defeat it

after all this time
I'm surprised at myself
for believing I still can

a wolf is still a wild animal
that cannot technically be tamed

you have an insatiable appetite
until I want or need something

then you're a pup again
teasing me with your
sweet innocent breath
soft kisses on my cheek

once again I succumb

how cold and lonely he must be

to never be full and satisfied
and never willing
to satisfy *me*

always feeding me breadcrumbs
in order to get your full meal

~ *supply*

can you for once
just want *me*
or am I not enough

~ *company*

when you're single
you wish for nothing
but love

you think you have it
and wish for nothing
but solitude

~ not love

others call us broken
maybe we are

but we seem to fit
perfectly together
don't we

smoothing the others
jagged edges

you like to remind me
we're all broken
to some degree

but are we willing
to help each other
rebuild — *heal*

you managed to stitch
together my broken heart

and yet
it still bleeds

I'm insignificant to you
until I'm not

then you howl at my
rejections to your
salacious requests

you catch more flies
with honey
my mother used
to tell me

I wonder what your mother
used to tell you

~ *it wasn't that*

love is either so lacking

    it's painful

or so abundant

    it's suffocating

I know it was you
yet you insist
on convincing me
it's me

with a stone face
you reply
I didn't say that

I pause
tell myself
I'm not crazy

you said it verbatim
I remind both of us

I just wanted you
to listen
to hear me
release my heart
upon your ears

instead I got
I told you so

do whatever you want

what forever feels like

to me
but please
don't do that

~ *gaslighting*

———♡———

it's not us — it's them
you like to convince me

is it *really*

much as we try
to shut it out

the negativity
seeps through
the cracks

~ infectious

she's brighter
when you're away

but the crown of loyalty
shimmers on the wall

then butterflies take flight
sprinkle fairy dust
into my eyes
instigating peace

when you're home
they fly away

~ *nightlight*

his tongue lashes out
and then retreats

slithering around the
carcass of your heart

before he swallows
you whole

12 years is a long time
to have the same thoughts
of fight or flight

I'm a type 5 personality
we're an interesting read

core fear — being helpless

sometimes it seems as if
you need me to be

helpless that is

you want me
to need you

I'm a master at
minimizing my needs

all you've ever wanted
was for me to need
your knowledge
your love
your time

you've never trusted me

why should I
trust *you*

do you know my biggest fear
any idea of the rambling thoughts
in my head throughout the day

can you tell me
what made me proud today
— *any* day

or are these things
overshadowed by
your own thoughts
and fears and dreams
and goals and — relevance

do you even know me anymore

how can you be
my only connection
my only safe priority

I cannot possibly
bring you happiness
if I am not free
to seek it myself

~ selfish

what will it take
to make you happy

I give you the moon
yet you long for
the stars surrounding it

I give you my heart
and you desire my soul

~ enough

—♡—

if you pay attention

the first time

they tell you

it will hurt less...

be a good little girl now

make my lunch
fetch my dinner
clean my house
raise my child

fuck me

now *fuck off!*

—♡—

I don't give a shit what you do.

The tone in your voice
told me you meant it.

I know you know
how much that hurts.

But I've grown.

I will not give you
the satisfaction
of an angry reaction.

You will never claim victory
upon witnessing tears
that you created.

May you reflect in my silence
because right at this moment —

I don't give a shit what you do either.

~ don't care

you crave my physical self

but are hesitant to understand

or even show an interest

in my thoughts

on any subject...

I would never want to lose you
but if I did — I'd be okay
without your disappointments
in me

I may not be everything
you had hoped for

but I always hoped
I was enough

you seem to hinder me
as much as inspire

why are mean men
such good lovers

you're a hypocrite

it's not cool for me
to express my frustrations

~ *noted*

such a neat little trick of yours
pretending like I'm invisible

I know you hear the rationale
forming from my lips

you see me standing here
though your eyes fixate
on the wall

you take your dig
and get the slightest
laceration allowed

your tongue nicks my skin
with pleasure in paper cuts
as I brush it off
with a warning

~ juvenile

snowflakes fall
like diamonds in the sky
as I plan the future
for you and I

wait — what was *that*

but we've come so far

my one consistency
outside of obligation

I don't want to be
obligated

we're both here
because it feels like
home

it is *home*
isn't it

yet you mock
my ability to live
— without you

because you're so
much better at it

~ diminishing

Is it too much to ask
to be chased for once?

I used to be able to
feel your every intention.

Or so I thought...

sex
sex
sex

do I not have *anything*
more to give you

spread my legs
silence my conversations
diminish any expectations

and then

you love me
every piece of me

~ *confusion*

awakening

——♡——

After all these years, it amazes me
that you still don't know, you're all
that's ever mattered to me...

——♡——

there's never a good time
for serious conversation

at least not if it doesn't
benefit or entertain you

heaven forbid I have any
grievances or concerns

other than what makes
my vagina wet

~ word porn

it was due to crash

things only go so well
for so long

wipe off the
crusted remnants
tell them
you will not
consume me

but sometimes
it's so thick
so abundantly
overwhelming

you're drowning
in the muck

finding it hard
to find the strength
to claw your way up

as it seeps
under your nails
engulfing every pore

packing your nostrils
and covering your eyes

slowly taking your
very last breath

~ *mud*

you always want to
discuss your concerns

there is never time
for mine

how to address them
deal with them
alleviate them

in the instant
I bring it up
you dismiss me

do you even know
what they *are*

can you name one thing
that would make *my*
life easier

and are you willing
to do the same

~ *unimportant*

I'm a mere vessel
drowning in your
fantasies

at your whim as you dream
of someone else

picture someone else
beneath you
feel yourself
inside of them

for once
can you just
pick me

how is it my fault
you're so hollow

must I play
someone else today

what is so wrong
with — *me*

~ real

I can play this game too
but I enjoy it more
than you

you're never alone
if you appreciate
being by yourself

you really only get angry
when it's pointed out
that you are not
the center
of the universe

~ *silent treatment*

I refuse to be your scapegoat
you made your choices
they were never mine to make
this truth is yours to bear
yet I endure the brunt
of the impact

~ excuses

you're mistaken

I exist to do more
than produce your
visual orgasms

the day that you fail
to strike a nerve
or make me shed a tear
should be of concern to you

love you
fuck you
clean your house
pay your bills

try to remain present
through each of your
mid-life crises

is it so wrong of me
to indulge myself while I try
with every shred of my being
to please you

~ needs

It was supposed to be a love story.

Maybe it's just another tragedy.

why am I always led
to believe something
is wrong with *me*

you're no longer
allowed to witness
the tears bleed
from my eyes

~ *deflection*

it is exhausting
sometimes devastating

more often than not
exhilarating
interesting
sexual
sensual
perverted
fun
honest

every tear
every smile
each insult
forcing reevaluation

every compliment
a reinforcement
of loyalty

taking the good and bad
of everything that we are
everything we were
to become

every single bit of it

I believed to be worth it

the sharp veins continue
to pierce through the
remaining scars
surrounding our hearts

no one has ever quite
captured me
like you

~ bonded

wash your face
tears don't look good
on you

I love you at your worst
yet you are the worst to me

~ heartless

Never underestimate those who can love and
feel into the cold black depths of the ocean.

I place my hand
on my bosom

it is mine
is it not

doesn't belong
to a child
or a man

my womb is mine
and I can create life

I can create life!
if I so choose

every single part
you crave of me

every single part
necessary for procreation
is mine and only mine
yet you wish for it
to be yours

I choose how and when
to share it

~ not property

sit down
smile

sit down
shut up
smile

no one cares
smile

they matter more
than you
smile

this is so fake

sit down
shut up
smile
act like you care

nobody else cares
what about me

it doesn't matter
sit down
shut up
smile

~ obey

I'm sorry my satisfaction
fails to satisfy you

I'm not a performance monkey

don't perform for me
you say

and yet you ask me
to do just that

~ unnatural

I am not your receptacle
accepting without remorse
your wants and
deviant desires

again I failed
to give you the performance
you desperately wanted
the one you fantasized about

even still
could you not find
any such enjoyment
where you had to treat me
like a second thought
like a slut in your porn

gratify yourself
all over my stomach
a thankless ejaculation

first time I showered
to prepare for you
and showered again
to rid myself of you

~ mechanical

I cannot be expected
to live up to your idea
of what you think
I should be

~ self

you just let me know
when you are ready
to take on some of this
juggling act

because I am
more than willing
to give up some
of the reigns

~ *it's heavy*

I see a mermaid in the slowly
passing clouds as the faint smell
of the lake tickles my nose
on a perfect august evening

alanis morissette calms my mind
reminding me I am more
than a wife — a mother
sister — daughter

I am me
I am free from the
rusty chains of my past
that haunt me relentlessly
tempting me
to take a step back

free from the preferred
guilt and victimization
free from the shiny new shackles
of obligation and condemnation
free to be at one — with peace

~ alone

she's high
don't mind her
you said when
I attempted to
voice my opinion

not like I think
or anything

don't swing your
tiny dick at me

you're like a third child
which I long for to mature
and eventually move out

why do men feel the need
to make women
feel so *inferior!*

~ *bullshit*

you've never seen
my potential
so centered on yourself
and your own

mock my ideas
remind me of my weakness
in comparison
to your physical strength
always competing

I'll never be
stronger
smarter
more agile
more enlightened

silly boy
as with every man
before you

I am a phoenix
and I shall rise

~ from ashes

I apologize that my needs
have gotten in the way of yours...

you used to criticize me
frankly — you still do

we always wish
we could correct
our past transgressions

but it's not possible

we can only move
forward

where do you
choose to remain

~ stuck

it's been so long
since I've loved myself

but you've loved me
this entire time
haven't you

I've never been alone
it's just always been
so lonely

~ unsure

———♡———

the rain pelts the leaves
hungry for comfort
as the ground
quenches her thirst

how I wish
to be both

~ *famished*

I apologize
let me comfort *you*

let me carry
all of the burden

pay your bills
fuck your cock

let me free you
of all sight
sound
responsibility

can't I share just a *bit*

it's so heavy

it's not a good time
i don't wanna talk rn
i gotta work in 30
it's saturday
it's my day off

nvm don't worry

~ I got it

the sun turns
the back of the trees
crimson at the end of the day

and I wonder
do my eyes deceive me
or am I really
seeing red

infuriating glow

~ anger

You say you don't follow your dreams —
because of me?

What a copout.

I think
therefore I am
I say

you laugh at
my ignorance
of the matrix

I think
therefore I am —
I see
I do
I love
I feel

nothing
it means nothing
it is nothing
we are but nothing

and yet
we are everything
we kill — we create
we destroy — we rebuild
we hate — we love
we bully — we include

we *are* everything

and yet we are nothing

~ so shallow

freedom

why are you so abrupt
so demanding
so exquisitely entitled

to be forceful with me
act as if you are better
than me
more intelligent
than me

I'm nothing special
but neither are you

~ get over yourself

what exactly are you sorry *for*

treating me like shit all week

giving me a false sense of security
by fucking me on thursday
then ignoring me again
for the next few days

or is it because I took
the lime light
wanted to share
my frustrations

I'm sorry
I didn't tell the story right
I'm sorry
I was repetitive

I'm sorry
the subject matter
didn't include you

~ corey's world

You are far from being the reason
I am not where I want to be.
But you *are* the reason
it is so much harder
for me to get there.

never been one to conform
I'm best when I'm free

you never could handle me
with my hair down and bra off
ingesting my medication of choice

pick your poison
and turn up the music
it's friday for god's sake

~ free spirit

when will men realize
women are actually
rulers of the world

we control the very thing
they all crave
and wish to possess

or at least have
available to them
at their discretion

always on their perverted minds
wanting to touch it
enter its welcoming warmth
begging for its smooth caress

knowing with fair warning
the doors can be closed and locked
at the first glimpse
of the need for retreat

~ *vagina*

he speaks to me
with a disgusted tone
I remain calm

his voice gets louder
words more vicious
I slowly try to walk away

the undiscernible words
echo through the walls

operation mitigation
only makes it worse

now he's yelling
I yell back

~ baited

I woke up with
a smile on my face
knowing we were
going to love each other
all day

at 10 am I stripped
down to my soul
until I realized
you locked yourself
in your room

you were fine
when you called me
on your way to work
fine when I text you
goodnight

slowly covering my
embarrassment as I redress
I wonder what it is
I've done wrong now

it's almost as if you
want me to be the bad guy
end this for both of us

~ *shame*

I no longer take baths

don't want to soak
in my misery

need the shower
to wash it the fuck away

I'm not your fucking
blow up doll

~ bitch on a shelf

I love you so much

it pains me to think
how often

I imagine my life

without you

~ *what if*

you'll never know
what it feels like
to be unsafe
or objectified

especially when I
am an object
to you

I'm not a doll

take me out of the box
and play with me

fuck me
lick me
touch me

put me back
on the shelf
until your next
compulsion

~ not barbie

We all deserve to be happy and loved.
Even if it is only through and with ourselves.

I'm allowed to exist
from beyond your needs

I am my own person
I have an identity far
removed from your own

I was not put on this earth
to be the center of your joy
satisfy your everything

I love you but I will never
need you and you
should never need me
you say I'm all you want
and expect me to only want you

no dreams or aspirations
no career goals or investments
no family — no friends
no other commitments

you either adjust what
you have to offer
or adjust your expectations

~ autonomy

your version of the truth
astounds me

I came to your room
while you dressed for work
asked if we could talk
about your son living
in our basement
who fails to respect me
just like you

you put your dick in my face
ignoring the weight of
my worries
as if you were trying
to be cute

I love you with every
burning inch of my soul
but I cannot stay with you
for the sake of my own sanity

~ last straw

I don't mistreat
I retaliate

you've never tried
to protect my heart

yet you wish
to possess it

~ property

a real man makes sure
you're not hungry
or cold
wanting or angry

a real man assures
your heart is whole
before asking for a piece
of your libido

a real man
will accept his downfalls
try to correct them
rather than side-step
deflect
and blame you

a real man will listen
to your concerns
comfort your wounds
and apologize if he created them
not pour salt or expand
upon them further

a real man will admit
when he's done wrong
rather than shame you

and blame you
for retaliation

a real man
would never make you
retaliate to begin with

~ a real man

you're not the only one
to blame

I've made certain things
acceptable when
they never should have been

now that I voice they're not
you're confused — and for that
I'm sorry

we could have been
so good together

it always felt so *right*

nothing about this
is right

you can't keep
hurting me
and pretend
you love me

~ *guilty*

I have cried for the last time
wondering if you'll notice

you never have
and you never will
notice

you never cared

always shook your hand
at any glimpse of feeling

any modicum of
responsibility or
accountability

I relieve you
of any commitment
you knew years ago
you would never be
able to adhere to

you never wanted this

I'm sorry
I made you feel
that you should

want this
or me

I free you

I give to you
what you so often
like to infer I took
without your permission

and I take back
what is rightfully mine

I love you
but I cannot
give up myself
to be your twisted version
of what you want me to be

~ individuality

you want me
to give myself freely to you

it's been the expectation
I have succumbed to
since the beginning

only the truth
remains stored away
hidden in my notebook

the one that holds
my thoughts and fears
questions and concerns
compressed to paper and ink

wanting
wishing
hoping
to unlock the voice
deep within my throat

pushing
screaming
to get out from under
the stacked bricks of guilt
pity and manipulation

~ escape

once you see something
for what it actually is

I mean really see it
at its core
at its true depth

it's a very hard thing
to unsee

~ woke

I'm not sure
which is more painful

the facade
initially created

or the truth
burrowing in your soul

~ future fake

I'm unsure where we go
from here

two months ago
one foot was out the door

of course you don't
want to give up
you're in a terrible
position

but nothing is the same

I'm not sure I can move past
this latest chaotic episode

you called me a petty ass bitch
your son called me a drunk

I spent weeks in silence
crying — thinking
trying to grab hold
of the same proverbial
safety net I always reach for

I try to let go
believe I'm ready

I feel the slow release
of the tentacles
until the grip strengthens
pulling me back under

I want to give myself to you

why after everything
does it feel so
superficial

I struggle to open my soul
for yet another disappointment

was any of this even real

years of manipulation
self-sacrifice
seemingly unwound

the self resurfaces
gasping for breath
reaching to the sky
for freedom

~ drowning

once the dust settles
all the good times
come flooding back

it's as if
they're the only ones
that ever existed

you contemplate
whether the good
outweighs the bad

and what if
they *do*

but what *if*
they never did

~ *rumination*

you took me to my
favorite restaurant today

we broke some bread
while I drank wine

I expressed how
enjoyable it was

until the ride home
when you went ape shit
on some random lady
just driving her drive

speed up
stop sign ahead

you screamed at me
for asking you
to slow down

enjoyable experience
you say

not today little girl

~ sike

I asked you
after we shared ourselves
most intimately

can you please be
a little more compassionate
can you be *understanding*

you responded by asking
can you please stop drinking

as if that was the source
of all our issues

my second glass of wine
didn't make you scream at me

my third beer didn't make you
call me a bitch

funny how when confronted
with things about yourself

I'm met with
what is wrong with me
what *I* need to change

like my mere existence
makes you who you are

how fucked up is that

~ projection

we planned dinner together
I finally made my macaroni
salad just like you asked

you joked about how long
it took me to comply
like you had waited
a lifetime

you came home
unhappy — depressed
you act as if I can never tell
your change in mood

I'm an empath
I feel *everything*

the burgers came out perfect

you slammed the mayo
into your bowl of pasta
murdering the noodles
as I layered the toppings
on my bun

i have to put so much
shit in here to make it

taste right
you said

ignoring the blatant discard
I continued to make my plate

i asked you not to put those
little things in there
you know i don't like them

then take them out
I respond
eat around them
I'm not making two batches

never knew celery
could become an enemy
of the state

after a few more
brushed off brash comments
I didn't allow to overcome me
you moved on to another tactic

pushing your way into my aura
and over taking my space you said
come on, get outta the way
instead of *looks great, thank you*

you fed me breadcrumbs
the past few days
satisfying me enough
to give myself to you again

showing my irritation
I move out of your way
the angry, vulgar words
heating the coil
in my spine

I brace myself
hold my ground as
peacefully as I can
without erupting

and then
you do erupt
flinging words from
your lips high in pitch
more forceful

an unrelenting battle cry
to be king
and I your whore

~ still not enough

I thought we would
grow old together

sadness fills my heart
knowing that my idea
of us and you
will never come
to fruition

I thought we would
be a power couple
conquering all the obstacles
that kept us from
the life we wanted

until the day I realized
the lives we wanted
were all too different

I actually had a plan
you say you're not
keeping me from it
so long as it's not
on *our* dollar or *your* time

still trying to figure out
how I lost sight of *my*

dollar and *my* time
I certainly never lost
sight of my dreams

I ask myself how it took
me 15 years to know
that mine were just
as valid as yours

~ goals

I don't even know
what to say
yet feel so much
has been left unsaid

I've been so invalidated
all these years
it feels strange looking
for it now
from anyone

it certainly won't
come from you

I crave it
like a drug addict
needing a fix

the sadness washes
over in ebbs and flows
like the ocean in sync
with the moon

I wonder if you feel pain
you appear fine
unaffected by the
hammer that just slammed

into your brick skull

taking another shot
at the ice block
around your heart

so many years
I tried to break
through the barrier
only to come out
bruised and broken

once healed and
on my feet
coming back
for another battle

~ it's over

I just wanted to hold you
you grabbed my ass
and my body reacted
though I didn't want it to

I kissed your lips
you grabbed me tighter

I pleaded
demanded...

you should learn
to love differently

~ intimacy

And one day she woke up
and remembered
who the fuck she was.

damn, sal

I think you were right
all those years ago

because any man
that has ever wanted
to have me

has never done so
for the right reasons

~ platinum

I cried last night
while I masturbated
I'm still unsure why

I didn't miss being
intimate with you

not that I would
call it intimacy

rather a mechanical
performance I
had to be
instructed upon

a fake porn video
you found
and wanted to
duplicate

there was never
true intimacy
not on your part

it was so cold
shallow — heartless

celia sinclair & e.m. handly

I try to recall the last time
I felt whole with you

no wonder I feel
so empty

you were so
full of shit
you never wanted...

~ just me

may 13th

my lucky number
or is it *unlucky*

jury's still out

today I suppose
it's in my favor

you invalidated me
yet again
and ironically
validated my decision
to leave

no longer insecure
that I've made a mistake

the entire universe
shifted within seconds
light speed — you're disgusted
with me
again

just two breaths before
I was all you still wanted

~ 13

it was ride or die

until I was shaken
realized I was mistaken
raised my sword
to self-preservation

and told myself
I would rather die
than ride any further
on this lame ass horse

~ ride or die

I don't know if
your ever knew
how to love me

I'm not even sure
if you can love
anything at all

celia sinclair & e.m. handly

I followed you to hell

you had no idea
how to climb out
but you liked it to
appear as if you did

you kept promising
the flames would subside
the blisters would heal

we could finally
live our lives
before it all
turned to dust

don't stoke the flames
don't let the oxygen in
smother the feelings

but the embers still burn
from deep under the ashes
awaiting their moment
to rise again

~ you lied

you never wanted peace

thrived on chaos
negative wave lengths
disturbing anything positive

it's so peaceful without you

while welcomed
it saddens me wondering
if you'll ever care
about anything

not for me — but for you

I do not need
your permission
to exist

I am allowed
to take up space

I am allowed
to speak
my mind

I am allowed
to be all
of *me*

and I declare
that I will exist
without you

although at one time
I wished we could exist
together...

~ don't need you

negativity grips your thoughts
like tentacles of an octopus
wrapped around your extremities
dragging you down into
the depths of darkness
until you drown

~ *healing*

I will never again
be placed in a box
like a barbie

your version of me
your molded creation

you groomed me
so clever of you

made me doubt
my own beliefs
think thoughts
that weren't mine

so clever of you
to casually sow the seeds
of doubt and confusion
make me question
my own reality

no longer under
your spell or control
your twisted definitions
or made-up perceptions

fifteen years later

once again
I am free

and I know that kills you

~ untamed

For more information, cool merchandise, and new releases, please visit www.emhandly.com